FIRE HD

8 & 10

A Technical Approach To Master Fire HD 8 & 10 In 2018

Leonard Eddison

terms of inattention or otherwise, by any usage or abuse of any policies, processes, or directions contained within is the solitary and utter responsibility of the recipient reader. Under no circumstances will any legal responsibility or blame be held against the publisher for any reparation, damages, or monetary loss due to the information herein, either directly or indirectly.

Respective authors own all copyrights not held by the publisher.

The information herein is offered for informational purposes solely, and is universal as so. The presentation of the information is without contract or any type of guarantee assurance.

The trademarks that are used are without any consent, and the publication of the trademark is without permission or backing by the trademark owner. All trademarks and brands within this book are for clarifying purposes only and are the owned by the owners themselves, not affiliated with this document.

TABLE OF CONTENTS

INTRODUCTION

Towards the end of 2011, Amazon announced that it was launching a tablet version of its popular e-book reading device: a tablet version of the globally known Amazon Kindle. This tablet version of the Kindle is known as the "Amazon Kindle Fire", and its announcement has attracted a lot of interest. Many computer enthusiasts want to know what this device has to offer in terms of features and other things. In response to the need for information, we now proceed to examine the key features of the Amazon Kindle tablet and to provide most of the information that the average person is likely to need about this gadget. The best way to go about that is by first looking at the hardware and then turning to its software.

KINDLE FIRE: THE HARDWARE

The key hardware features of the Amazon Kindle tablet include:

1. Its 1 GHz Dual core processor allows the tablet to execute various computing tasks at remarkably fast speeds without the latency associated with computing devices that come with sub-gigahertz processors.

2. 512 MB RAM: allows the Amazon Kindle Fire to handle multiple tasks simultaneously without losing efficiency.

3. Its multi-touch screen makes for a convenient (and one would say classy) user interface.

4. 8GB of secondary storage has more than enough storage space for the apps and data the average tablet computer user is likely to need.

The 8 GB is shared out so that 3 GB can be used for storage of apps, even as 5 GB is available for data storage (anything from songs to movies and e-books).

5. Multi-device compatibility is possible through a series of ports that make it possible to connect the Kindle Fire to USB devices, desktop computers, laptops, SD cards and so on.

KINDLE FIRE: THE SOFTWARE

The key software features of the Amazon Kindle Fire include:

1. It's Android operating system platform that makes it possible for Amazon Kindle Fire users to install and run numerous apps developed for use on the popular (and open source) Android platform.

2. Default email-syncing app makes it possible for Kindle Fire users to get all their emails from various Webmail systems (Yahoo Mail, Gmail, Hotmail and so on) in one single inbox.

3. E-book reading app makes it possible for people who wish to use the Kindle Fire primarily as an e-book reading device to do so conveniently.

However one chooses to look at it, the Amazon Kindle Fire comes across as a decent tablet computer, one that comes with pretty much all functions expected from a tablet computing device. It becomes even more alluring when one learns its price, which is half the average price of other tablet computers on the market.

NEW KINDLE FIRE E-READER TABLET

Amazon recently came up to par with their release of the new Kindle Fire e-reader tablet. Many have been waiting for the upgraded version of the previous Kindle and Amazon finally answered by releasing the 7 inch, full colored, and WiFi capable Kindle Fire.

The Kindle Fire comes fully equipped with a 7-inch full colored screen with 1024x600 resolutions. Along with the beautiful full colored screen, Amazon also installed a dual-core processor inside of the tablet.

Although Amazon has not released what speed the processor is currently clocked at, this makes a much better alternative to the Nook Color's single core 800 megahertz clocked processor. This ensures faster web browsing capabilities for the Kindle Fire tablet, but

Amazon went the extra mile by incorporating their own web browser called the Amazon Silk.

AMAZON SILK - THE SMART BROWSER

Another browser you say? Don't be fooled because the Amazon Silk is totally worth it. In plain English, what the Amazon Silk browser does is take the processing capabilities of your Kindle Fire device and also the processing capabilities of the Amazon Cloud system. What this means is that it will split the task and memory required when web browsing and decides whether the device will process it or the cloud space system will process it. This equals greater web browsing speed and efficiency and really lives up to its "Silk" name. Amazon decided to name its browser Silk because a thread of silk is an invisible but strong connection between two things, which in this case is your Kindle Fire tablet and the Amazon Cloud system.

INCREDIBLE AMOUNTS OF CONTENT FOR YOUR PLEASURE

Another great feature Amazon is offering the tablet users is their library of 18 million movies, songs, books, magazines, and TV shows for purchase. Amazon's Library makes it seem like the Barnes and Noble 2.5 Million library look like nothing. But if you still can't get enough content, Amazon is also offering applications like Pandora and Netflix to have instant streaming movies and music capabilities to your device, with a subscription fee of course.

KINDLE FIRE VS. NOOK COLOR

Everything technical about both devices is like a splitting image of each other in terms of size, screen, and display. But what sets apart the Fire and the Nook Color is the support the Kindle has the Nook Color tablet and its blazing fast dual-core processor. After this Kindle Fire Review, it's safe to say that this device is far better than its competitor: the Nook Color tablet.

FEATURES THAT YOU WILL ENJOY

Some of the features that you will enjoy when you get this device are such as built-in email application, which enables you to constantly communicate with business associates, friends, and family. This device has been applied in business aspects such as internet marketing including email marketing. Kindle Fire also uses Amazon's Whisper sync technology, which enables a user access eBooks, Videos and TV stations.

With the free cloud storage, you are able to access the Amazon's cloud services and stream data including books, music, and movies. Through the Amazon cloud drive, you can gain access to over 10 million songs from the music library and this means that Kindle Fire is an ultimate entertainment device. For the parents and kids, this is both a learning resource tool as well as entertainment spots.

With over 1000 illustrated children's books, your kids will be always busy improving their learning skills. The bestsellers' books including comic and cookbooks are streamed via this device and on average there are about 1 million books you can access. It seems that Kindle Fire does not only offer home related applications but also business apps. With increasing need for Internet use at home and in work, this device offers ultra-fast web browsing features, which are ideal for business applications.

Businesses need speed and power in their web applications and with the Amazon cloud servers, they are able to enhance web presence with high-speed internet connectivity and reduced server downtimes. When you get this tablet, you can enjoy most of the features that are found in Apple's iPad.

In order to support all these multifunctional features, Kindle Fire is designed with an advanced dual-core processor, which guarantees fast, powerful and reliable performance. The stunning physical features impress many people and the color touch-screen brings out lively movies, children's books and magazines in great colors.

Its durability is enhanced by its design materials. The Fire is made of Gorilla Glass, a material that is resistant to cracks, scratches, and damage. This also improves its aesthetic beauty. The back of the Fire has a rubber texture, which prevents the tablet from slipping and falling. The rubber-like material creates firm grips when holding the device. If you would like to get a product that is equivalent to the Apple's iPad, then Kindle Fire is the right device. It has been praised for high performance.

WHAT CAN A KINDLE FIRE DO?

There are a lot of misconceptions surrounding the Kindle Fire and what it can do. Because of its name, its association with the Amazon Kindle

Store and past iterations of the Kindle e-book reader, many people thinks of it as simply an e-book reader. It's far more than that.

It's a fully functioning tablet computer running the Android operating system depending on the version you choose and it's one of the more reasonably priced tablets on the market today.

It's a great e-book reader as one would expect, but it can do far more besides just reading e-books. It would be more aptly described as a media tablet.

So What Can the Kindle Fire Do?

Because the Kindle Fire is a fully functioning tablet computer, the possibilities are almost infinite. If there's an app for it, you can do it.

There are literally thousands of apps available for the tablet on the Amazon Appstore for Android. Many of which are capable of being played on the standard Kindle Fire and the very latest high-end games can be played on the Kindle Fire HD.

Games aren't the only app available for the Kindle Fire. Many apps have far more practical applications. There are finance apps, real estate apps, educational apps, word processor apps, music apps, weather apps, shopping apps. The list is almost endless. There are even apps that can teach you how to pilot a plane.

In fact, it would be easier to answer the question "what can't the Kindle Fire do?" as that would be a far smaller list and could be summed up in one paragraph.

What the Kindle Fire can do fresh out of the box:

1. Video playback

The Kindle Fire is a very good video player. Its 7-inch screen is more than enough screen for watching a movie without needing to squint your eyes to see the lead actress. Because you hold the screen in close proximity to your eyes, it actually feels as though you are watching a cinema screen rather than a 7-inch screen. Those who feel that they would like a larger screen to view movies on and read e-books will be glad to know an 8.9 -10 inches is now available.

The video playback quality is very impressive. Though the file sizes can be relatively small, it can be comparable to watching a Blu-Ray movie because of the screen size.

A typical full-length movie file, if you use MP4 format, can be anywhere between 300-800mb, with most weighing in at around 400mb. This would allow you to store between 15-20 movies for the 8GB model. The Kindle Fire has 8GB, 16GB and 32GB models available. So at approximately 400MB, you will be able to store 35-40 and 75-80 movies respectively on the 16GB and 32GB model, making allowances for the space taken up by the operating system.

This can, of course, be extended by using the fantastic Amazon Cloud Storage which is free to all Kindle Fire users. The cloud storage is unlimited, so the amount of movies you can store and stream to your device is infinite. It's worth noting, however, that only movies purchased through Amazon can be streamed via cloud storage onto your device. For your own movies, you will need to load them onto the device yourself.

If you go for Amazon Prime membership, there will be thousands of movies and TV shows available to be streamed for free. So if you like movies; Prime Instant Video is well worth the money.

2. Music playback

The Kindle Fire is a very good music player. The MP3 files available on Amazon are of very high quality. The dual driver speakers and the headphones provided are very good. To get the most out of their music, many music junkies will want to invest in a high-quality, top of the range set of headphones or external speakers. But it has to be said, the music playback as standard (through the speakers) is top-notch.

Given a file size of 5MB, the standard Kindle will be able to store around 1,600 songs, which is more than enough. Obviously, it can be extended to an infinite amount using the cloud storage mentioned earlier.

3. As an e-book reader

The file sizes for books are not that small, often just a few hundred kilobytes for even the largest novel, so many thousands of books can be stored on the 8GB model. For the 16GB and 32GB model, you would be able to store more books than many humans will read in their entire lives.

Amazon Prime membership will also mean that you can borrow an ebook every month, with a choice of hundreds of thousands of books on offer.

4. Web browsing

The Kindle Fire is a very good web browser, thanks to its excellent touchscreen. The screen is also large enough to be able to browse without it becoming fiddly. The Silk Browser is a very competent browser, which actually seems to load many web pages better than Apple's Safari.

Web browsing requires a Wi-Fi connection. 4G LTE Wireless is available on the Kindle Fire HD 8.9" but this is the top-of-the-line model.

The Kindle Fire is possibly the most under-rated tablet around at the moment. It certainly manages to beat other tablets available in its price range. And the answer to the question "what can the Kindle Fire do?" would probably surprise many people, who think it's just a simple e-book reader.

CHAPTER ONE
WHAT TO EXPECT FROM
A KINDLE FIRE TABLET

It probably comes as no surprise that Amazon is set to launch the Kindle Fire Tablet in November. One big question seems to be how it compares to the iPad. Maybe the question should be: how will it be used or what do you really need from a Tablet. Many times shiny new objects blind us, and we make poor choices. There is no doubt that the iPad is an impressive shiny toy! But will you really use its many features? So, is it a need, will its many features really be used or is it just another gadget that we want? Now let's consider the alternative: the Kindle Fire Tablet is small and can easily be carried in a pocket or a purse. It can be held in one hand, movies can be viewed in true widescreen on the 7" color Touchscreen, and it is well made. It is extremely user-friendly, and at $199 it is more affordable than the iPad. On the other hand, it does not have the same features as the iPad, but this is where you really need to get honest and think about personal needs when purchasing a Tablet. So what is missing from the Kindle Fire? It does not have a camera which means no video chatting. It does not have Bluetooth technology which means no wireless connection to a separate keyboard. It does not have access to the thousands of apps found on the iPad.

The Fire does focus on Amazon content. If your primary use will be reading books and magazines, watching movies, checking email and browsing the Web, this may be the ideal tool. It does have access to some games and apps.

.

CHAPTER TWO
INFORMATION ON THE DEVICE'S CONSTRUCTION AND OPERATING SYSTEM

Anyone who studies history understands that to look back is to look forward, and it seems construction technology follows suit. As construction is rapidly moving into a digital-first world, companies are seeing major shifts in the ways technology helps them reinvent personnel and equipment management and even use virtual and augmented reality to concive, construct and maintain their buildings. The speedy pace of innovation has heads spinning, often leaving companies feeling a sense of fear from a lack of control. But as technology pushes forward to modernize construction, could an innovation from the past provide construction with the next big thing that helps everyone stay in control? You've kicked it off with a big cup of Joe at the office watering hole. There's a buzz in the room, and one phrase, in particular, that seems to be on everyone's minds: construction operating systems. We get it; keeping up with industry lingo is exhausting. You just mastered the cloud. You use it, understand it, and can mention it in a sentence without a millennial rolling their eyes at you. And now this?

To your credit, the term is so new that we don't blame you if you don't quite understand it yet. But one thing is clear: it's not just the latest trend; it's the newest era in construction—which means it's only a matter of time before your boss tries to engage you in a conversation on the topic. So, instead of walking into your next meeting with no response, be invaluable with answers.

THINGS TO KNOW

What is a construction operating system?

A construction operating system is a term for the central, cloud-based software that helps connect every single point solution, device, and person across your entire construction company from bidding to closeout.

How does it work?

Using an Open Application Platform Interface (Open API), all of your favorite point solutions— regardless of brand—are connected. Your project management, bid management, quality and safety, and job costing solutions work harmoniously under the same roof. Then, a construction operating system takes the data from all of these applications and gives you real-time, easily-digestible, and trend able insights from one centralized hub.

What is an open API?

Essentially, it's Rosetta stone for software code that allows two programs to communicate and interact freely with one another (with the help of a translator, so to speak). For example, with an Open API, your project management and accounting solutions can speak the same language and bilaterally exchange information. When your systems communicate seamlessly with one another, your field teams don't have to wait for office staff to confirm with their accounting software that they are within the budget. Because the field teams already have that information on their project management solution.

What is data?

You collect data on a daily basis just by doing your job. Each time you complete a daily log, make an observation or submit a change order, you are collecting data. With thousands of these submitted on a single job site every day, you're left with an overwhelming amount of information or data. A construction operating system automatically does the math for you and presents you with the results rather than the equations.

And data is the currency to executives and owners because it allows them to make informed decisions about their project based on facts, not guesswork. So, opting out of interpreting your data is like lighting a stack of cash on fire.

If I want a construction operating system, do I need to upgrade my devices?

Absolutely not! The beauty of cloud-based software is that you never need to buy new hardware (aka devices) in order to upgrade your software. It's all done automatically for you. And not just once a year but...Every. Single. Day.

I'm not sure if I have a Construction Operating System. How can I check?

This is an extremely new concept in the construction industry. Currently, there are very few companies that offer real, unconditional Open APIs. Because of this, chances are you might not have a construction operating system yet. Check to see if your software solutions offer limitless integration possibilities and access to a truly high-level overview of all of your applications in one dashboard. If you don't have either of those, you don't have a construction operating system.

Now for the ultimate question: What's the big deal?

Well, it's a huge deal. For the first time in history, the lifecycle of construction has the potential to be unified and effortlessly predictive. Imagine having the ability to accurately forecast next year's profits before you start a single build, or prevent accidents before they happen. That's the kind of predictability that construction operating systems have to offer. That's the stuff your boss really wants to know. So, commit the above answers to memory. It's a step in the right direction of providing your company with the keys to the future of construction. But don't stop there. Make yourself invaluable to your company by continuing to research the ins and outs of construction operating systems.

OPERATING SYSTEM UNIFICATION

Construction needs unification, and a construction operating system is what the industry should be looking to develop. To build the projects of the future, construction will need to connect people, technology (think: device agnostic) and software. An operating system, providing that connectivity, would remove the friction of development, data extraction, and usability from construction and in turn, give construction companies much more than increased collaboration by establishing unity, uniformity, data security and eye-opening insights.

From the architect and engineer to the project manager on the job site and the subcontractor pouring the concrete, imagine everyone working off the same data, seamlessly connected and contributing to construction's evolving landscape. But first, it's important to understand the history of this technology.

ERP SYSTEMS IN CONSTRUCTION

In the late 1980s and early 1990s, ERP systems entered the purview of companies who wanted a "one-stop shop" to combine their functions, streamline operations and aggregate important data. With complex business needs, these ERP solutions provided off-the-shelf solutions that required businesses to tailor them to fit their unique business practices. In many cases, companies were forced to re-engineer their business processes to accommodate the logic of the software. It became a necessary and arduous task for companies to streamline data flow throughout their organizations. Construction fell victim to the ERP system, having to force unique, carefully orchestrated processes into the shackles of limited software functionality. The virtual "shoe" never really fit. How could a system built for a less-chaotic industry meet the needs of an industry as complex as construction?

Way to solutions

Born from frustration, point solutions were then developed to fill the gaps in areas ERP systems (even those patched together with easy-break code) just couldn't perform. Originally built to solve one particular problem, when new or multiple problems arise, new point solutions are born. Given that construction uncovers about 100 or more new "problems" a day, these singular solutions quickly become plural—opening the door to bigger management issues. All of these singular solutions, living in every corner of the business, house important information on which companies need to share or collaborate. In addition, multiple stakeholders need to have access to multiple point solutions and are forced to duplicate data so that every system has the most up-to-date information. This, in turn, opens the door to the next issue. How can companies cobble together all these singular point solutions so that collaborators can collaborate, data can flow between all the systems and issues can be properly tracked?

Integrated systems allow users to perform various unique functions with bi-directional data flow so that users can collaborate, share information, track key data and only have to enter information once. Using an integrated platform helps construction reduce data entry mistakes, breaks down communication issues and streamlines processes.

However, many solutions were not built to integrate. In the fast-paced world of construction technology, developers often have a single-minded approach to building their solutions. If the solution was not built to be extensible (i.e., have an open API), it is limited in usability when trying to integrate with systems it wasn't built for. So are these two steps forward and one step backward when it comes to construction technology?

Not literally of course. But if construction looks back to the early 1980s, there was a tremendous shift in technology that opened up the world of computing: the operating system. Made famous by Micro-soft (before the hyphen dropped), a "universal" operating system allowed competing vendors to license the operating system and then create hardware of their own, in which a hardware and software ecosystem evolved. Since the operating system could connect the hardware to software developed for various singular tasks like creating Word documents, or Excel spreadsheets (or apps for project management), companies didn't have to worry about building out complex "brain" code and reinventing the wheel. They could connect software designed for their needs and count on a standardized operating behavior that laid the foundation for their success. Finding and installing apps for the Fire Advice for managing your own content on the device

FOR T.V

However, Amazon's user interface isn't always the friendliest, and many of the Fire's better features remain hidden away. We've listed the nine features of Amazon's Fire TV Stick and a set-top box that you really need to know about.

1. Learn to use the shortcut menu

Fed up with navigating to "Settings" or diving through menus to turn off your Fire TV or Fire TV stick? Well, Amazon has actually included a shortcut menu for speedy navigation. Press and hold the home button to open up a pop-up menu with quick select for Power, Mirroring or Settings. Simple.

2. Use your Amazon Tablet as a second screen

If you have an Amazon Fire HD or HDX tablet, you can actually use it as a second screen when watching content on Amazon Prime Instant or for navigating around your Fire Stick. You can also push content to your tablet, meaning you can enjoy your Fire TV even if someone else is using the TV. As with everything else on Amazon's media box, it's pretty easy to set up. Head to Settings | Second Screen and then turn it on. Just make sure your device and your Fire tablet are on the same wireless network.

3. Mirror your Fire Tablet to your TV

As with Google's Chrome cast, you can mirror your Amazon Fire phone or tablet to your TV. To do so, make sure your tablet is on the same network as your Fire TV Stick or box and head to Settings | Display & Sounds | Display Mirroring on both your TV and tablet.

4. Enable Parental Controls to keep your kids safe

Amazon allows you to place Parental Controls on your Amazon Prime Instant account or apps installed onto your Fire TV device. Not only does this keep your kids from accessing inappropriate content, but it also means you shouldn't end up with any surprise payments. While a device-level setting for Parental Controls will cover all Amazon content on your device, you'll still need to set one individually for other apps such as Netflix.

5. Expand your internal storage for games and apps

As standard, Amazon's Fire TV comes with 8GB of internal storage. While that may sound reasonable, any serious Fire TV user will discover that it fills up all too quickly. Thankfully the latest update to the Amazon Fire TV set-top box allows you to plug in a USB stick and transfer over your games and apps. You'll need to make sure it's a USB 3 stick formatted to FAT32 (otherwise Fire TV will wipe everything when it formats it) if you want to expand your storage. Once plugged in, just go to Settings | Applications | Manage Installed Applications to transfer content to a USB stick. External hard drives will not work.

CHOOSING THE RIGHT DEVICE FOR YOU

First of all, let's explain the key differences between the Fire TV box and its more affordable sibling, the Fire TV Stick. While the Fire TV box may be twice the price, it's a lot more powerful and has access to more games as a result. You'll see some slow-down in 3D games at times with the Stick, for example, as it uses a remedial dual-core CPU. It's fine if you want a cheap media machine, but it is no console-replacer.

The Fire TV Box is a lot more powerful, with a 64-bit MediaTek 8173C CPU that has two Cortex-A72 cores and two Cortex-A53 cores – equivalent to the power of a very good mid-range phone.

It also has more connections, with an Ethernet port, optical audio output, and a USB. Finally, it can output in 4K where the Stick's max resolution is 1080p.

The "all-new" 2017 Fire Stick has a much more powerful processor and is absolutely fine for streaming TV shows and films.

However, if you've not yet bought a Fire TV device and want to play games, you're better off with the box version. It supports many more games because it has that extra power on tap – the likes of Minecraft: Pocket Edition, Asphalt 8 and many others simply don't work on the dual-core Fire TV stick, even if you sideload them.

More on that later, but now it's time to look at how you can make the most of your Fire TV.

1. Find shows on Netflix and player with voice control

When the Amazon Fire TV with mic first launched, it would only look up Amazon goodies:

movies from Amazon and apps from the Amazon Appstore. This was annoyingly limited, but now it's actually quite useful as it'll look up videos on Netflix and iPlayer, too, and we'd expect Spotify support to be incoming soon.

PHONE/TABLET

The Amazon Fire tablet range continues to rise in popularity, gaining ground in what is described as a "declining market". Is it all about the price? Are you missing out on important features found on Samsung and Apple tablets if you opt for Amazon?

1. Install google play store and get android apps

In fact, it's really simple to install the Google Play Store and expand the library of apps and games you can install on your Amazon Fire tablet. Over the years, this has been rather complicated, but if your device is running Fire OS 5.x, you'll be able to install the files you need via the device's browser. Because Amazon's mobile operating system is based on Android, the tablets are compatible with almost all Android apps and games.

2. Expand the default storage

One of the shortcomings of the low-end Amazon Fire tablets is the limited storage. If you own the 8GB model, you're looking at around 5GB to play with (the rest stores the operating system). That's not much, especially if you're keen to use the device to play games, or store videos for viewing later. The answer is to expand the storage with a microSD card. Many people don't realize this, but the Amazon Fire tablet has a micros storage card slot on the side.

All you need to do is purchase a suitable expansion card, and then while the tablet is switched off, insert it into the slot. You can use micros cards of up to 256 GB in the Amazon Fire. Once this is done, boot up the tablet again. The micros card should be detected, so follow the instructions to format it. Many apps can be installed to the micros card. Existing apps can be moved to the microSD card via Settings > Storage > Move Apps to SD Card to move supported apps. Music, too, can be migrated to the expanded storage device; go to Music > Menu > Settings > Transfer All Offline Music, then Transfer All to SD Card.

3. Watch your own movies

With additional storage installed on your Amazon Fire tablet, you can enjoy its benefits as a portable media device. Sure, it's a good way to make sure your tablet doesn't run out of space, but you can also use the storage to save movies, TV shows and music from your own collection. Taking a long train journey? Simply copy your favorite movies to your tablet and enjoy them as you ride. You can do this by connecting the Amazon Fire tablet to your computer via USB. Once detected, browse to the microSD card storage and copy the video file from your PC. To view the video, go to Video > Library and open the hamburger menu. Scroll to Personal Videos and tap your synced personal media will be listed here.

As long as it is in the right format, your video will play. (MP4, MKV, 3GP, M4V, and WEBM should all work. There is no support for AVI videos.)

4. Get rid of pesky ads and special offers

If you have the cheapest version of the Amazon Fire tablet, it's likely that you have to contend with adverts. Lots of them, particularly on the lock screen. So, what do you do about it? One option is to pay to have these removed via Amazon. However, it's also possible manually block ads from hitting your Amazon Fire tablet with the help of a special utility.

5. Perform office tasks

PC or laptop is out of action? Need a mobile working solution? Amazingly, the Amazon Fire is an ideal tool for mobile working. With built-in Bluetooth and a number of office apps available, it's really easy to set up, too.

Various portable Bluetooth keyboards are available that run with almost any tablet or phone. Simply pairing one of these to your Amazon Fire tablet will put you on the road to office functionality. You'll find a bunch of these devices on Amazon; perhaps an ultra-portable, foldable keyboard? Once that's done, find the office apps that you need on Amazon's App Store or the Google Play Store.

Microsoft Office apps, Google's Docs and Sheets, and a number of other office tools are available. Worried about things like copy and paste? Don't be. This functionality is built in. The Amazon Fire also comes with a number of productivity apps already built in, such as email, calendar, and calculator apps.

6. Watch movies anywhere

You know that you can copy movies to your Amazon Fire. You probably also know that you can watch movies and TV shows via the Amazon Instant Video app. Perhaps you have an

Amazon Prime subscription and gain the benefit of some free streaming movies and shows.

7. Stand up

With the right case or a useful stand, you can make your Amazon Fire tablet stand up.

8. Screen record and screenshots

Recording the Amazon Fire's screen is possible with third-party tools. Depending on which model you own, however, the results may not be satisfactory. Low-end 8GB models tend not to respond well to screen recorder apps, resulting in poor-quality recordings.

Need to take a screenshot of your Amazon Fire's display? Whether you're playing games or using the browser, taking a screenshot might prove useful.

It might be to illustrate an article like this or to get technical support for a problem you're facing.

To capture a screenshot, hold the Power button and Volume Down at the same time. (Note: Volume Down's position depends on the orientation of the tablet.) After 2-3 seconds, your device will capture the image on the screen and save it to storage. From here, you can edit or share as needed.

16 things you probably had no clue you could do

Amazon's Fire TV platform comprises streaming set-top boxes and sticks, including the latest Amazon Fire TV 4K.

To help you get the most out of it, as well as any older Amazon streaming device, we've rounded up a selection of tips and tricks worth knowing. We've mentioned tips like how to change your device name so it's easier to decipher which is which (should you own several of the same devices and want to push content to a specific one). Also, we've included tricks like how to restart your box using the Amazon Fire TV remote.

Expand your internal storage

Amazon's Fire TV provides 8GB of internal storage for apps, music, and other files you want to save locally. But did you know the Amazon Fire TV also allows you to plug in a USB stick and transfer over content? You just need a USB 3 stick (formatted to FAT32) to expand your storage. Also, while it's plugged in, go to Settings > Applications > Manage Installed Applications to transfer content to the USB stick.

Change your device name

Amazon assigns names to its devices, such as the Amazon Echo, Fire TV, Fire TV 4K, and

Fire TV Stick. If you own several of the same devices though (like maybe three Amazon Fire TV 4K boxes), it'll be hard to decipher which is which when you buy apps or content and want to deliver that stuff to a specific device. An easy solution is to change the names of all your Amazon devices. From a desktop computer, go to your Amazon account (drop-down menu under your name), then find the Manage Your Content and Devices page, and go to Your Devices tab. You might at this point be asked to sign into Amazon once more in order to verify your identity. You can then click on any device (followed by the Edit link) to change its name to something more recognizable.

Connect Bluetooth headphones

The Fire TV set-top boxes support Bluetooth headphone connectivity. With your headphones in hand, go to Settings > Controllers and Bluetooth Devices > Other Bluetooth Devices on your Fire TV. The box should then automatically find and connect to the headphones. Voila!

Turn your Amazon Fire tablet into a second screen

Amazon allows its higher-end tablets, such as the Amazon Fire HD or Fire HDX tablet, to become second screens while you're watching content on Amazon Prime Instant (or for navigation purposes with your Fire TV Stick). You can also push content from your streaming device to your tablet, so you can use your Fire TV even if someone else is watching TV at the same time. From your Fire TV, go to Settings, then Second Screen, and toggle on the feature.

Both devices must be on the same network, though.

Mirror your mobile device on your TV

Just like Apple's Airplay feature, you can mirror your Amazon Fire phone or tablet to your TV.

The Fire TV and Fire TV Stick support Mira cast, a Wi-Fi solution for showing multimedia across multiple screens. So, if you're playing video on a mobile device, you can display it on your HDTV via Fire TV. Supported devices include the Fire Phone, Fire HDX tablet, Windows 8.1 and up computers, and any device running Android 4.2 (Jelly Bean) or higher. The device has to be on the same Wi-Fi network as your Fire TV.

From there, go to Settings > Display and Sounds > Enable Display Mirroring on the Fire TV. You may have to go to your mobile device settings as well to enable Mira cast. Alternatively, hold the Home button on the Fire TV remote and select "Mirroring." Push any button on the remote to stop.

Go here to learn about Mira cast.

Remove apps from your home screen

You can actually change around your home screen by removing the featured apps under your Recently Used tab. Just navigate to the app you want to remove, and then below it - next to "More info" - you'll see a "Remove from recent" option. Click it to remove it from home screen. It will reappear under this section the next time you use the app, though.

Set a custom screensaver

To set your own image as the Fire TV's screens craver, upload an image to the Amazon Cloud Drive account linked to your Fire TV, then go to the "Photos" tab on your Fire TV, and find the image you want to set as a screensaver. You can do this with an entire album of images too. Just select 'Set as Screen Saver', and then you can change your style settings, such as the slide style, slide speed, etc. Alternatively, you can also set your Screen Saver settings by pressing the Home button on the remote and select Settings > System > Screen Saver.

Install apps from Amazon's website

You can install apps directly from Amazon's website. Simply browse Amazon's online catalog, then go to the app you want, and you'll be able to purchase it and push it directly to your

Fire TV device after purchase (as long as your streaming device is linked to your Amazon account).

Use the shortcut menu

Amazon offers a shortcut menu for speedy navigation: press and holds the home button on the remote to open up a pop-up menu, and you'll see quick options for Power, Mirroring or Settings.

• Use the remote to restart

You can restart the Fire TV devices with the Fire TV remote. Go to Settings > System > Restart.

You can also simultaneously press and hold the Play button and Select button for about five seconds. Simples.

• Repair the remote

Should you remote get disconnected, repair it to the Fire TV or Fire TV Stick by holding down the home button for up to 10 seconds.

• Cast from YouTube

You don't need Google Chrome cast to cast videos from the YouTube app on your mobile device to your TV. Just load the YouTube app on Fire TV and then do the same with the app on Android or iOS. From there, tap the Cast icon in the YouTube mobile app, and that's it. Again, make sure your devices are all on the same Wi-Fi network.

Delete ASAP Info

Amazon's ASAP feature learns what Amazon movies and shows you like so they start instantly. But if you want to delete the entire feature's saved info on you, go to Settings >

Applications > Amazon Video. Then clear the data and clear the cache. You can also clear the cache for other apps.

Delete Voice Recordings

Amazon also stores recordings of everything you voice search through your Fire TV, but you can delete the recordings. From a desktop computer, go to your Amazon account (drop-down menu under your name), then find the Manage Your Content and Devices page, and go to Your Devices tab. You might at this point be asked to sign into Amazon once more in order to verify your identity. You can then click on any device, select Manage Voice Recordings, and then click Delete.

Voice search on the Fire TV Stick

The Fire TV Stick does not have that same voice search option that's on the Fire TV box.

But you can buy the $29.99 Voice Remote for Amazon Fire TV and Fire TV Stick to get it. Or, download the Fire TV remote app for Android or iOS. Your phone will need to be on the same Wi-Fi network as the Amazon Fire TV device to work. The name of the Fire TV will appear on the Smartphone screen. Click it, then punch in the code that appears on the screen, and you'll have full control.

Enable Parental Controls

You can enable Parental Controls on your on your Fire TV device, allowing you to block purchases and restrict access to Amazon movies, TV shows, games, apps, photos, and more. This will stop your kids from making surprise purchases as well as accessing inappropriate content. To use parental controls and purchase restrictions, you need to set a 5-digit Amazon Video PIN for your account using an Amazon remote or the Fire TV Remote App. Go here to learn more about how to set up a PIN. Keep in mind, after you enable Parental Controls, most actions related to content viewing, purchasing, or changing settings require you to enter your PIN.

FIRE TABLET TIPS AND TRICKS

Note: These tips and tricks were tested on an Amazon Fire HD 8 (2016) but should work on the latest Fire tablets.

1. Hard reset your tablet

If your tablet freezes or seems to crash, all you have to do is press and hold the power button for 20 seconds and the device will really shut down. Once you give it a few moments of rest, turn it back on by holding the power button. You'll get the boot-up animation and all should be well.

2. Access quick settings and notifications

The easiest way to change settings on your Fire is via Quick Settings. Go to your home screen and swipe down from the top. You will see a menu that lets you adjust the Screen Brightness, enable Blue Shade, set the device to Do Not Disturb, or open the full Settings menu, etc. The area below the Quick Settings menu also serves as your notifications shade, where you can see and dismiss notifications.

CHAPTER THREE
HOW TO SET UP YOUR
FIRE TABLET FOR MOST
EFFICIENT USE

At the time you turn the Fire tablet on for the first time, you see a series of screens that help you set up and register the device. Don't worry: There aren't many questions, and you know all the answers. At some point during this setup procedure, you may be prompted to plug your adapter in, if your battery charge is low. You may also be notified that the latest Fire operating system is downloading and that you have to wait for that process to complete before you can move forward. In most cases, Amazon will have pre-registered your Amazon account to the device so you shouldn't have to register it yourself. However, if you don't have an Amazon account, you'll get a chance to create one during setup. During the setup procedure you'll also make choices about your language and country, time zone, and the Wi-Fi connection you'll use to go online.

Tips- After you work your way through the setup prompts, you see a Welcome screen. Tap Get Started to see the first of several screens that help you learn to navigate the Fire tablet by swiping left, up, and down on its screen. At the end of the series, on the screen titled Congratulations, tap Finish to go to the Fire tablet Home screen.

In most cases, Amazon will have pre-registered your Amazon account to the device so you shouldn't have to register it yourself. However, if you don't have an Amazon account, you'll get a chance to create one during setup. During the setup procedure you'll also make choices about your language and country, time zone, and the Wi-Fi connection you'll use to go online.

Simple steps

INITIAL SETUP

Usually, there will be enough battery power to get through the setup process and install a few apps. But it's also a good idea to attach the bundled USB cable and mains charger and allow the battery to fully charge. When you first turn on a Fire tablet, it will ask to choose a language and a region. Tap Continue and you'll see the Connect to Wi-Fi screen. The password is usually on a sticker on your router, or sometimes on a removable card.

Choose the correct network and type the password, which will be case-sensitive.

The tablet will check if there are any software updates, download and then install them.

Next, you'll be prompted to enter your Amazon account details to register the tablet: email address and password. This is necessary in the same way it is on a Google or Apple phone: you can't install any apps or games or any other content from Amazon (such as books, videos and more) without an Amazon account.

Doing so also allows you to install apps from any web browser, rather than on the tablet itself. Note if you don't have an Amazon account, you can tap the 'New to Amazon' link to create an account.

If you've had a Fire tablet before, you may be offered the option to restore a backup. You can restore the most recent backup to save the hassle of installing apps and games. Plus all your settings will be as you set them, including email accounts, bookmarks and more. Swipe down from the top of the screen to see the Quick Settings panel where you can adjust screen brightness, change user profiles, enable flight mode and various other things. The cog icon takes you to the full menu of settings.

CHAPTER FOUR
WHERE IS YOUTUBE AND THE GOOGLE PLAY STORE?

Although based on Android, Fire tablets are not Google Android tablets. This means there are no Google apps at all, including YouTube.

You can fire up the Silk Browser and go to the relevant websites (Gmail.com, YouTube.com etc) to use Google services, but you can also download a third-party YouTube app and use the built-in E-mail and Contacts apps to access your Gmail account.

To download the YouTube app, tap on Appstore and then tap the magnifying glass icon (top right) and type YouTube. There are many apps, but this one is our favorite, by the developer 'YouTube.com'.

CHAPTER FIVE
HOW TO USE ALEXA?

After you've got an Amazon Echo, Fire TV or Fire tablet, here's how to use Alexa. We explain what to say and how to say it and also how to use multi-room music on the Echo.

Most people are used to talk to their phones, even if it's only to ask Siri or Cortana to set an alarm or timer. Alexa is Amazon's voice assistant, built into its range of Echo devices, but you'll also find Alexa in other speakers as well as on Amazon's Fire TV media streamer and tablets including the £49 Fire.

Here we'll explain how to talk to Alexa, what you can ask her and how to use the multi-room music capability. There are also many funny things she can say.

Like any good digital assistant, you can speak to Alexa using natural language. In the US she can recognize individual voices and provide information specific to that person (such as what's on their calendar) but she doesn't need training: she will respond to anyone's voice.

When speaking, you don't have to say "Alexa" and wait for a response. Just look and check that the LED ring has lit up, and carry on speaking.

Bear in mind that unlike Siri and Google Assistant, Alexa can't take multiple commands at once.

NEW ALEXA FEATURES

These are the latest skills Alexa has learned:

Fire TV control- From 27 February, if you own both a Fire TV and Amazon Echo you can use Alexa to play videos: no remote controller required. The feature has been available in the US for a while, but now UK owners can join in the fun. If you have just one Fire TV, you merely need to ask Alexa (on your Echo) a question involving the Fire TV, such as "Alexa, play the Grand Tour on my Fire TV". All being well, it should pair automatically and you'll have hands-free control over searching for shows, fast-forwarding and more. Many Fire TVs come with an Alexa remote, but if you have any Amazon Echo and any generation of Fire TV or Fire TV Stick, you'll now be able to use Alexa without pressing and holding a button.

• CORTANA

Soon - no date is confirmed - the virtual assistant built into Windows 10, Cortana, will be able to communicate with Alexa.

AMAZON FIRE HD 8 VS. FIRE HD 10 — WHICH SHOULD YOU GO FOR?

Amazon's not overly flashy about it, but it's got a couple of the better Android tablets available today. That's perhaps damning with faint praise but hears me out. The Fire HD 8 and Fire HD 10 perhaps get you the most bangs for your buck. Certainly, that's true for Android-based tablets, and you could well argue it's true of any tablet anywhere. The basics: As the names imply, Amazon has an 8-inch tablet and a 10-inch tablet. They're both running the "Fire OS" operating system, which is Amazon's own version of Android. They get apps from the Amazon Appstore and have full access to Amazon Music, Books, Video, Movies and everything else Amazon does. And both are inexpensive. Not relatively inexpensive, but downright cheap. But they're cheap without really feeling cheap, know?

What else do you need, right?

OK, you need to choose between the two. We can help. Here's what I'd compare to the Amazon Fire HD 8 and Fire HD 10.

Comparing Fire HD prices

As you'd expect, the larger Fire HD cost more than the smaller. But there's more to break down here. Each is available with "special offers," which means there are ads on the lock screen and in the notification pull-down. They don't actually bother me too much. But they don't really jack up the price of the hardware that much if you choose to go the other route.

So, on the whole, the smaller Fire HD 8 is a little less than half as expensive as the larger

Fire HD 10. But you also get more for your money if you get the model with the lower storage, as the price per gigabyte is a bit lower. Couple that with the fact that you can add in a micros card to extend the storage, and you wouldn't be wrong to go for the lower of the two sizes.

Which one's better to use?

For the most part, using the Fire HD 8 and Fire HD 10 gives you a relatively similar experience. They both run the same Fire OS operating system (slightly different version numbers, but whatever). But the Fire HD 10 has better internals. It's got a better processor and more RAM, and it definitely runs things a little more smoothly — though still not anything earth-shattering — than the Fire HD 8. These are still very much mid-range tablets, but the Fire HD 10 won't leave you wondering what's going on behind the scenes as much. But for me, the bigger difference is in the displays.

Sure, we're talking an 8-inch display versus a 10-inch display. But we're also talking differences in resolutions. The Fire HD 8 tops out at 720p, while the Fire HD 10 comes in at 1080p. Along with that higher resolution, the Fire HD 10's display density is about 15 percent higher than the Fire HD 8. And I've found that dark colors are definitely darker on the Fire HD 10. That makes pretty much everything look better. And that's key for the Fire HD 10 because it's ultimately the better device for watching video. And video is a key component of Amazon's strategy these days.

CHAPTER SIX
HOW TO WATCH VIDEO
ON FIRE HD?

STREAM OR DOWNLOAD VIDEOS

You can stream movies or TV shows on your Kindle Fire from Amazon Video. Help for Kindle Fire (2nd Generation), Kindle Fire HD" (2nd Generation), and Kindle Fire HD 8.9" (2nd Generation).

Before you stream a movie or TV show, make sure your Kindle Fire is connected to a wireless network. To learn more, go to Connect to Wi-Fi.

Note: Not all videos available in the Amazon Video store are available in the Prime Video catalog. With an eligible Amazon Prime membership, you can instantly stream Prime

Videos to your Kindle Fire or download selected Prime Videos to watch later.

From Home, tap Videos, and then swipe from the left edge of the screen to open the navigation panel.

1. Tap Your Video Library, and then tap Cloud

2. Select the Movies or TV tabs to locate the titles you want to stream or download:

3. To stream a video, tap the Watch Now button or the play icon.

4. To download your video, tap the Download button or the arrow icon.

If you experience an error while using Amazon Video, visit the Amazon Video Errors help section.

Tip: You can connect your Kindle Fire HD to a high-definition television or monitor using a micro-HDMI cable. To connect your Kindle Fire to your display, make sure both your Kindle Fire HD and display are turned off and then plug the micro-HDMI cable into the micro-HDMI port on your Kindle Fire HD. Connect the other end of the micro-HDMI cable to the HDMI port on your television or monitor, and then turn on your display and Kindle Fire HD. Once connected, you can watch your videos, view your photos, and play your games on a larger screen.

Your new Kindle Fire is an awesome piece of technology, isn't it? You can play movies on it, view your photos, listen to MP3s and, of course, read newspapers, magazines, and books!

When you think about what it can do you can't help but be amazed at the level of technology is contained in such a small device, can you?

Even if you've only had it for a very short time you are probably already starting to wonder how you ever managed without it. It will, no doubt, soon be your constant companion at home, on the train, bus plane or when visiting friends and family out. It will go everywhere with you and be infrequent and regular use.

You'll be able to watch movies of your choice without disturbing the rest of your family at home.

Basically, you'll most likely take it with you wherever you go!

CHAPTER SEVEN
GOOD REASONS TO
CONSIDER A KINDLE FIRE
TABLET

Like any other tech device, there are pros and cons of each. Consumers would be best served doing their homework and determining how they plan to use the device in order to make sure they're making the right decision. With tablet computers and e-readers, there are a number of different makes and models to choose from, with the Kindle Fire providing another option.

The Amazon Kindle Fire may not be the right choice for many, but there are a number of advantages that shoppers should consider before they make their final decision.

1. Price

At $199, it's reasonably priced compared with other tablets on the market. One of the most popular tablets right now is the iPad by Apple. Current iPod models cost more than twice as much as this Amazon tablet, so it makes sense to determine if that extra cost is worth it based on your particular needs.

2. Operating system

Running on the Android operating system, consumers with experience running other devices utilizing Android will have some level of familiarity with how the OS works.

3. Size

Its 7.5" long and 4.7" wide. This is a bit smaller than some other tablets and similar in size to other versions of the Kindle. If you're looking to carry your tablet around with you, the smaller size of the Kindle Fire may be an advantage over other larger tablets like the iPad. For women, the Kindle Fire will fit nicely in larger purses or it can simply be carried like a small book if necessary.

4. Amazon

Since it's sold by Amazon, consumers know that they can trust the company that they'll be buying from. With Amazon being one of the largest retailers online, consumers can be comfortable knowing they'll get quality customer service if an online business that many of us have used for other online transactions. Other firms like Apple also offer excellent customer service, but if you're looking at some tablets that are being offered by small unknown companies, consumers should be careful before they make a purchase and determine if the product being offered will perform as advertised.

5. Compatibility with Other Devices

With the number of Android-based smartphones on the market, considering the Kindle Fire as your tablet of choice just means that it will be another extension to the programs you are probably already familiar with. If you use Gmail for your email or the Google Calendar software, both of which are offered online for free, you will easily be able to sync your data between your desktop email and calendar, you've smartphone and the Kindle Fire if you choose to go with this as your tablet.

6. Software

Apple's iPad runs iOS proprietary software, and it's quite limited in terms of what the user can change or install on the machine. The Kindle Fire offers more versatility, as it uses the open source operative system Android. If you are looking for gifts for somebody who likes Linux and Android, the Kindle Fire is a great candidate.

7. Storage

The iPad offers from 16GB to 64GB internal storage, compared with the 8GB offered by the Kindle. However, since both offer Wi-Fi connectivity it's relatively easy to offset this by just storing your files elsewhere. The Fire is heavily tailored towards using Amazon Cloud offering, clearly offsetting the reduced storage space compared with the iPad.

8. Battery life

Both devices can go for days without charging, and the Amazon Kindle offers up to 8h battery while reading. This is more than enough for most users, even in long trips.

9. Games and Apps

The iPad has been on the market for longer, and so it has a large following of loyal developers that have created apps for about anything you can dream off. On the other hand, the Kindle is tailored to consuming Amazon content, either music, videos or books, and it delivers just fine on that. Considering that Amazon is one of the largest marketplaces for this kind of consumer items, Fire owners aren't going to run out of things to read or see any time soon.

SO, IS THE KINDLE FIRE A GOOD IPAD ALTERNATIVE?

Considering the price, the Kindle Fire is a great alternative compared to the iPad for people who don't feel like spending a lot of money or want a very portable device to access their music, videos, and books on the go.

CHAPTER EIGHT
HOW TO FIND AN
AMAZING KINDLE FIRE
DEAL

Finding a great Kindle Fire deal can make all the difference when it comes to buying one of these devices. Since they are fairly new to the market, they are extremely popular. There are a lot of different retailers that sell them, so you can purchase from just about anywhere.

HOW CAN YOU SHOP ONLINE FOR A GREAT KINDLE FIRE DEAL?

When shopping online you will have the advantage of being able to comparison shop. The Kindle Fire price is just $199 when it's not on sale, so it's very affordable. Finding a lower price than this is going to mean more money in your pocket. Just because you save money doesn't mean the device will work any differently, so there's no reason not to look for some great deals. When looking around online, consider all retailers that sell these. Amazon is the first place you might want to check out. One of their most popular deals is where you can get a few dollars off the price when using a certain type of credit card to purchase it with.

Amazon also has a marketplace with private sellers who offer their used and new devices up for sale.

HOW TO USE KINDLE FIRE?

So you got yourself a Kindle Fire? Congratulations! But do you know how to use

Kindle Fire? If no, a few tips will start you off. If yes fine, but may you also get something you may have missed along. In my view, you are now holding one of the best tablets on the market. Forget about iPad, the Fire is the real thing, and you will know that with time.

You now need to start taking advantage of your device. The first thing is to Set up & Sync. After connecting the Fire to your Amazon account settings, you need to sync it with your existing services and media libraries.

The Fire lacks email client. To access email, your only option is to use the browser. However, you can download an email application for your device. There is a dedicated Yahoo mail client which is for free. Assuming you are on Gmail, Hotmail and/or other providers, your best bet is

Enhanced Mail, but you will have to pay around $10.

To make a calendar accessible to your device, there is an application which you could purchase for around $6.0. The beauty of paid applications is that it syncs with Google calendar.

You can import your books from another application to your Fire. You do this by pulling Archives in your Kindle application. For a new Kindle reader, you can select and download free books for a start by selecting the store button.

You can get music on your device by uploading your library to Amazon Cloud Drive first. From there, you can get your music on your Kindle Fire.

You also need to learn how to use Kindle Fire to download and pin application you designate as favorites. I am assuming that you are a cyber fan. There is lots of mouthwatering stuff you come along all the time. The temptation to download some is irresistible. If you always find yourself downloading applications, Kindle Fire makes it even easier.

There are applications for games, news, entertainment, messengers, and others. Some of these are free, but others you need to pay. The important thing to remember is to check whether the applications have been formatted for smaller screens. Once you have downloaded the application you feel they are a must in optimizing your Kindle Fire experience, pin the ones you are likely to use most on the bottom carousel.

Heard of Amazon prime? It's important in this guide on how to use the Fire. Well, Amazon offers lots of goodies with Amazon Prime. The first thing is to sign up. With Amazon prime, you get the following: free shipping for 2 days, access to their library on your Kindle, and you can borrow one book every month. The first month after signing up is free. Later, though, a subscription is required.

CHAPTER NINE
GREAT APPS FOR KINDLE FIRE

So you just bought a Kindle Fire and you have checked out a few books, maybe listened to some music, watched a video or two and of course, you browsed the web. Now what? Luckily there are tons and tons of applications created by third parties that you can download onto your new Fire. There are thousands of them out there, but I have drilled down and found what I consider to be the very best 3 apps out of all of those. Follow along as I tell you about these 3 Kindle Fire apps and why I think they are the best.

1. Badass Battery Monitor. If I could only have one app, I would have this one. It gives you so

many great details about what is going on with your battery, it is unreal. This should come included with the Fire it is so extensive. It will tell you how much time you have left as well as what percentage of the battery you have left until you will need to charge again. The app also shows you what apps and usage is taking up all of the battery and draining it the fastest. It is extremely helpful and is a great insight into your inner workings of the Fire.

2. CalenGoo. If you want to connect your Google Calendar to your Kindle Fire, this is the best app to do it. You can sync your calendar, easily swipe between days, weeks, and months to see future appointments and plans. The best calendar, hands down.

3. Pulse. Typical RSS readers are not in style anymore. Pulse takes it up a notch and provides an extremely visually appealing way to stay current with all of your favorite blogs and news sources. You can set up various tabs so if you want finance news on one tab, sports news on another tab, and funny webcomics on another tab, you can do that.

There you go! If you are only going to get a few apps, these are a good mix. Some productivity, some fun, and a great utility to help you to monitor your Fire's battery usage. Hopefully, you will check out these apps for Kindle Fire soon. Enjoy your Fire!

KINDLE FIRE FREE APPS THROUGH AMAZON

The Kindle Fire may still be second to Apple's iPad, but it is still the best tablet PC on the market at a price point that makes it accessible to almost everyone. The Kindle Fire gives users great access to Kindle Fire apps and Kindle Fire free apps.

You have an array of Kindle Fire apps at your fingertips through Amazon App Store for Android. No matter what your interest is, the Fire can give you the choices you need to get the most from your Kindle Fire device. Let's take a look at some of the choices you have to select from:

1. Sports & Games: Keep up to date on your baseball scores with MLB app and many other sports alike. Kindle gives you access to some of the best games on the market such as the top seller Angry Birds which sells for a nominal fee of $0.99 for the download. You can find games of the past such as Tetris and Pac-Man. Another

popular download is Scrabble which sells for $2.99 for the download. Kindle Fire free apps also include Solitaire Free Pack and Words for Friends to name a few.

2. Foodies: If you are a foodie you will enjoy the different apps that are available. From food magazines to recipe applications you can find it for the Fire. From magazines, such as Bon Appetit and Cooking Light to apps such as Everyday Vegan and Wine Snob. There is something here for everyone including free apps such as Urban Spoon, Mighty Grocery Shopping List, and Calorific.

3. Music & Movies: This tablet PC was made for listening to your favorite music and streaming your favorite movies and videos. With access to Netflix, you can choose to buy or rent a movie at your leisure. Besides being able to listen to your

music, you can take advantage of the Pandora app to listen to playlists that fit your listening preferences. Don't count the Fire out for business though; you can get an array of business applications such as LinkedIn, Evernote, and Documents to Go. All these apps are offered free for your use!

There is a nice mix of paid and free apps with this device in every category. Like all free app's, there are mobile marketing opportunities that will appear in the app itself as you use it. This allows the marketer to offer you the application free. While most will allow you to upgrade for a small fee to remove the ads; mobile marketing is similar to watching a commercial between TV shows. Click Kindle Fire Free and Paid Apps for more.

<u>*CONCLUSION*</u>

The Kindle Fire, Should I Get One?

In a world of countless technologically innovative gadgets, it is sometimes difficult to keep pace with the changes in designs and models that you are certain to encounter almost daily. This is especially true of the many handheld units that are available. In recent times the name Kindle Fire has been gaining popularity. But there are still many people who would ask the question what is the Kindle Fire? Technology buffs will sum up the Kindle Fire as one of the most current and impressive devices for electronic entertainment and data sharing. In fact, it is the latest version of Amazon's Kindle eBook reader. It is a small interactive multi-touch display unit with Wi-Fi accessibility offers users a window to a world of limitless entertainment and communicative options.

Small and Powerful

The unit is small but it has amazing capabilities. The web tablet uses Android as its operating system. One of its awe-inspiring features is its screen resolution of 166ppi. This coupled with its wide screen, which allows you to see the images on the screen with amazing clarity and sharpness, and at pretty much the same size as you would on a larger device.

When you consider that the color depth of the unit has the capacity to facilitate as many as 16.2 million colors you understand how magnificent the images on the screen must appear.

Multiple Uses

Designed for multiple uses, the handy device has become quite the rave among technocrats across the globe. With this 'mini tablet' users can browse the web, read books, listen to music, watch videos, check emails and even play games. Web browsing and email access on the unit are supported by the Kindle Fire's pre-installed Silk browser and its 802.11b/g/n wireless connectivity.

Kindle Fire owners also benefit from its 8-gigabyte integrated flash memory. You can use roughly 6 gigabytes of this for storage. This is what facilitates the unit's ability to store so many files. In fact, the unit can store up to 6, 000 books, 800 songs or 80 apps and ten movies. The standard home screen icons represent the categories, books, newsstand, apps, docs, videos, music and web.

Bang for your buck

The device is so popular that its name is commonplace in some of the most remote places across the globe. With an average price of 200 dollars, the device is obviously well worth its price especially when one considers the many features.

In addition, customers who purchase the unit from Amazon get it delivered with log in settings already enabled. All that is required is that you enter your login information to get access to the features of your Kindle Fire. Upon login, you will find that you have instant access to all the eBooks that you have purchased or music that you have downloaded via Amazon.

Essentially, the Kindle Fire tablet gives users top-notch convenience, comfort, and entertainment in a compact and easy to handle the format. It should be comforting for buyers to note also that the device comes with a one year manufacturer's warranty